Friendship

by Janice Musante

Friends Forever Card

Best friends bring out the best in each other. Share the joy of true friendship with a gorgeous card and matching envelope.

SIZE: Card: 5" x 5", Envelope 6" x 6¼"

MATERIALS:
Grafix Dura-Lar .007 • Decorative papers • Ribbon • Clear glass microbeads • Pressed flowers • Stickers • Pearl brad • *Tsukineko* Lavender Brilliance ink • Double-sided tape • Adhesive

INSTRUCTIONS:

Card: Cut Dura-Lar, fold to form card and ink edges. Cut out 6 pressed flowers in squares. Cover with double-sided tape and sprinkle glass beads over each flower. Shake off excess. Adhere 5 to card. Attach ribbon to the corner with a brad. • Adhere 4 sentiment stickers inside the card, positioning them beneath a clear space so that you can read them from the card front.

Envelope: Use a template to cut out an envelope from two-sided paper. Fold and adhere to form the envelope. • Adhere rub-on, ribbons, and beaded flower.

How to Make Cards from Clear Film

1. Measure and mark clear sheets with a ball point pen or grease pen. The ink will wipe off easily.

2. Cut acrylic with sturdy craft scissors. Punch holes with a 1/4" hand punch or with a Crop-A-Dile.

3. Score clear acrylic with the pointed end of a bone folder. Fold on the score line then flatten with the side of the bone folder.

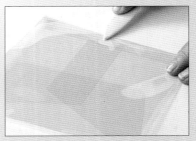

4. Envelope - pattern on page 14. Score, bend and flatten the folds with a bone folder. Glue the side and bottom flaps with clear adhesive.

Thoughts to Remember

by Janice Musante

Thanks Floral Card

From grateful me to wonderful you, Thanks. Elegant swirls and a pretty flower express your appreciation.

SIZE: 5½" x 5½"
Envelope: 6" x 6¼"
TIPS: Using two-sided paper eliminates the need to line this attractive envelope. Use a sticker to close the envelope when presenting this card.
MATERIALS:
Grafix Clear Dura-Lar .007 • Rub-ons • Decorative papers • Paper flower with pebble brad • Ribbon • White Brad • Blue daisy • *Tsukineko* StazOn White ink • Die cuts
INSTRUCTIONS:
Card: Cut Dura-Lar, fold to form card and ink edges. • Adhere rub-ons, ribbon, flowers and brad. • Cut papers to fit. Ink the edges and adhere to the inside of the card.
Envelope: Use the envelope template to form an envelope. Fold and adhere edges. • Adhere die cuts and brad.

"B - Birthday"

Celebrate a special day with a special card. Silvery black swirls and the initial give this card a classic appearance without being too frilly.

SIZE: 5" x 5, Envelope: 6" x 6¼"
MATERIALS:
Grafix Clear Dura-Lar .007 • Decorative papers • Die cut • Rub-on • Flower • Brad • *Tsukineko* VersaMagic ink (Brown, Peach) • Ribbon • Adhesive
INSTRUCTIONS:
Cut Dura-Lar, fold to form card and ink edges with Peach. • Cut 4 letters "B"; 2 of these cut in reverse. Ink edges with Brown • Center and adhere 1 letter "B" to the front of the card.
• Open the card and adhere a reverse letter "B" to this letter, facing outward and aligned.
• Apply rub-ons to the front of the card. Adhere a small, peach colored flower and a folded ribbon to the front of the card with a brad along the lower right edge of the "B". Trim ribbon edges and apply "irthday" sticker onto ribbon. Adhere "Happy" onto letter "B". • Center a letter "B" on the inside of the card and adhere. Apply rub-ons. Adhere reverse letter "B" to the backside and facing outward, matching up B's.

"H - Happy" Birthday

Simple embellishments combine in a graceful greeting that everyone will appreciate.

SIZE: 5" x 5", Envelope 6" x 6¼"
MATERIALS:
Grafix Clear Dura-Lar .007 • Die cut • Decorative papers • Silk flower • Rub-ons • Brad • *Tsukineko* VersaMagic inks (Brown, Lime Green, Peach) • Adhesive
INSTRUCTIONS:
Cut Dura-Lar, fold to form card and ink edges with Peach. • Cut 4 letters "H" with 2 cut in reverse. Ink edges with Brown.
• Center and adhere 1 letter "H" to the front of the card. Apply rub-on doodles. Cut a small tag from Dura-Lar, ink edges with Lime Green and apply rub-on "birthday" to the tag. Adhere the flower and tag to the lower, right edge of the letter "H" with a brad. Rub-on "appy" in the center of the "H". • Adhere the reverse letter "H" facing outward aligning it with the cover "H". • Center and adhere one letter "H" to the inside of the card. Rub-on doodles. • Adhere the reverse letter "H" facing outward aligning with the other "H".

Enjoy the Journey Tag

Perfect to celebrate a graduation, personal achievement or job promotion, this tag will be a treasured keepsake.

SIZE: Tag: 2½" x 5", Envelope: 3½" x 5½"

MATERIALS:
Grafix Clear Dura-Lar .005 or .007 • Cardstock • Paper flower • Large pebble brad • Die cut machine and tag dies • Printed transparency • Rub-on doodles • 3 rhinestones • Ribbon • Rub-ons • *Tsukineko* Black StazOn ink • Hole punch • Adhesive

INSTRUCTIONS:

"Joy" Tag Envelope: Die cut 2 tags and ink edges. • Adhere tags together. • Wrap and adhere ribbon at the top and bottom of the tag. Adhere "Enjoy the Journey" sentiment, and apply rub-ons. Attach flower with a large pebble brad. Adhere rhinestones.

Tag: Die cut a cardstock tag slightly smaller than the envelope. Adhere transparency, ribbon, and rub-ons. • Punch a hole in the top center of the tag. Thread ribbons, knot and trim the edges.

Hide It - You can hide adhesives or elements by placing a photo or cardstock on the back. This is a great place to add a special sentiment. Or simply place a large flower or stickers on the back.

Beautiful Greetings

by Janice Musante

Mom Card

Why wait for Mother's Day? Send a loving sentiment to Mom "just because".

SIZE: 5½" x 5½", Envelope: 6" x 6¼"

MATERIALS:

Grafix Clear Dura-Lar 005 • Decorative papers • White envelope • Self-adhesive pearls • Silk flowers • Rub-ons • Die cut • *Tsukineko* ink (StazOn Black, VersaMagic Peach)

INSTRUCTIONS:

Card: Cut Dura-Lar, fold to form card and ink the edges.
• Die cut 2 of the letter "m" using 2-sided patterned paper. Center and adhere one letter "m" to the card front and one to the inside aligning both letters. Adhere flowers randomly across the card front. Adhere pearls to flower centers.
• Cut out a small Dura-Lar tag, ink edges with Black and rub-on doodles. Adhere the tag under one flower, at the bottom right edge of the letter "m". • Randomly rub-on doodles so that when the card is closed the doodles complement one another and do not overlap.

Envelope: Apply rub-ons, die cut leaves, flowers and brads to one corner of the envelope.

Dragonfly Card

Absolutely gorgeous and brimming with activity, this picturesque card is perfect for the nature lover in your family.

SIZE: 5" x 6", Envelope: 6" x 6¼"

MATERIALS:

Grafix Clear Dura-Lar .007 • Decorative papers • Stickers • Pebble brad • Blue daisy • Rub-on doodles • *Tsukineko* VersaMagic Persimmon chalk ink • ⅛" hole punch • Adhesive

INSTRUCTIONS:

Card: Cut Dura-Lar, fold to form card and ink edges. • Trim papers and adhere inside the card. • Adhere clear sentiment inside the card. • Adhere rub-on doodles, dragonfly and firefly stickers on the front of the card.
• Punch a hole in the lower, left side of the card front and attach the blue daisy with the large pebble brad.

Envelope: Cut a strip of matching paper and adhere at the bottom edge of the envelope front. Cut and layer additional pieces of coordinating papers as desired.
Adhere the "Travel" sentiment and firefly sticker.

Simple Pleasures Card

The small, everyday joys of life are meant to be shared. This card is so quick to make you can send out several... one to each of your friends.

SIZE: 4" x 5½", Envelope: 6" x 6¼"

MATERIALS:
Grafix Clear Dura-Lar 007 • Photo • Cardstock • Rub-ons • Paper flowers • Pearl brad • Ribbon • Die cut machine and card die • *Tsukineko* White StazOn ink

INSTRUCTIONS:
Die cut a clear Dura-Lar window card and ink the edges. • Mount a photo onto White cardstock and adhere inside the card. Apply rub-on 'Simple pleasures' inside the card and attach flowers and ribbon with a brad. Apply leaf rub-ons • Apply rub-on doodles to card front.

Baby Tag

Here's a fun tag for a baby shower gift.

SIZE: 2¾" x 5½"

MATERIALS:
Grafix Clear Dura-Lar .007 • Decorative papers • Rub-ons • Ribbon • Letter stickers • Die cut machine and tag die • *Tsukineko* Black StazOn ink • Hole punch • Adhesive

INSTRUCTIONS:
From clear Dura-Lar, die cut 2 tags and ink the edges. Apply rub-ons to front of tag. Cut a letter B from double-sided paper and adhere between the tags. Punch a hole in the top of the tag. Thread ribbons through hole and tie a knot. Adhere rhinestone to front of tag.

Add Clear Embellishments - Add clear acrylic tags and accents inside your envelopes. These add fabulous dimension. You can mark or rub on designs to embellish this clear item also.

Print Photos on Clear - Print your photos on *Grafix* Transparency Film (for inkjet printers). The photo will show twice, once on the front of the card and once again on the flip side.

Add Sheer Ribbon - Sheer looks great when attached to a clear card. Stitch or glue Organza ribbon for a fabulous look.

Transparency Overlays - Secure transparency images with brads or eyelets. *Hambly* Transparency screen prints are perfect for this. TIP: *Grafix* makes Transparency film so you can print out your images, words and photos on a computer.

Timeless Card

Savor the memories of a timeless friend with a card that will become a treasure.

SIZE: 5¼" x 5½"

Envelope: 6" x 6¼"

MATERIALS:

Grafix Dura-Lar .007 • Decorative papers • Rub-ons • Stickers • Paper flower • Pebble brad • Silk flower • *Tsukineko* StazOn inks (Black, Peach) • ⅛" hole punch • Adhesives

INSTRUCTIONS:

Card: Cut Dura-Lar, fold to form card and ink edges. • Trim paper, ink edges and adhere stickers and rub-ons, then adhere to the inside center of the card. • Apply rub-ons and epoxy sentiment sticker to the card front. Attach flowers with a brad.

"B for Baby" Card

Monogram letters are hot design elements, so this card is sure to be a favorite. Send it as a birth announcement or with a gift at the shower.

SIZE: 5" x 5¼", Envelope: 6" x 6¼"

MATERIALS:

Grafix Dura-Lar .005 • Decorative paper • Ribbon • Die cut • Silk flower • Brad • Rub-on doodles • Clear alphabet tags • Lime Green embroidery floss • *Tsukineko* Lime Green VersaMagic ink • *Making Memories* Brown ink and inkpad • Sewing needle • Double-sided tape • Adhesive

INSTRUCTIONS:

Card: Cut Dura-Lar, fold to form card and ink edges. • Die cut 4 of the letter "B" with 2 cut in reverse. Center and adhere one letter "B" to the card front and apply rub-ons. On the card inside, center and adhere another letter B, face up. Line up and adhere the reverse B's on the backside of each page. • Attach a folded ribbon and flower to the upper corner of the B on the front of the card with a brad. Tie floss through the letter tags and adhere to card.

Envelope: Make an envelope from Dura-Lar using template. Firmly crease all edges so that the envelope lays right when adhered and the flap closes. Fold and tape sides and edges. Add ribbon to the sides.

Heartfelt Greetings

by Janice Musante

Cow Tag

We mooved! No one will forget your new address when you announce it with a tag that will have everyone chuckling.

SIZE: 3½" x 5½"

MATERIALS:

Grafix Clear Dura-Lar .005 or .007 • Decorative papers • Felt cow • Ribbons • Die cut machine and tag die • Rub-ons (doodles and Black lettering) • Chipboard heart • *Tsukineko* Black StazOn ink • Black pen • ⅛" hole punch • Adhesive

INSTRUCTIONS:

From clear Dura-Lar die cut 2 tags and ink edges. Apply rub-ons. • Punch a hole into the top of the tags. Tie ribbons through both tags. • Cover the chipboard heart with paper, ink the edges and adhere to tag. • Thread ribbon through the hole in the cow, knot and trim. Adhere cow to tag. • Apply rub-on Black lettering "We've Mooved". Trim decorative papers to fit between the tags. Ink edges and adhere between the tags.

Sheep Tag

Light hearted and whimsical, this "baad" sheep brings birthday wishes.

SIZE: 3½" x 5½"

MATERIALS:

Grafix Clear Dura-Lar .007 • Decorative papers • Felt sheep • Die cut machine and tag die • Ribbons • Stickers • Rub-ons • *Tsukineko* Black StazOn ink • Black pen • ⅛" hole punch • Adhesive

INSTRUCTIONS:

From clear Dura-Lar die cut 2 tags and ink edges. Apply rub-ons. • Punch a hole into the top of the tags. Tie ribbons through both tags. • Thread ribbon through the hole in the sheep, knot and trim. Adhere sheep to tag. • Apply rub-ons and stickers. Trim decorative papers to fit between the tags. Ink the edges and adhere between the tags.

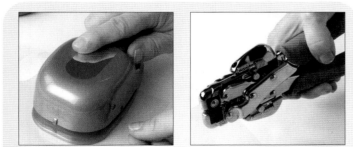

Punch Holes in Clear Pages - Use a hand punch (A Whale of a Punch works great) to make decorative holes in clear cards. Use the holes as little windows to something fun.

Make Holes in Clear Pages - Use a Crop-a-Dile tool to make holes in clear cards without cracking or bending. Attach ribbon, brads, eyelets and items in the holes.

Family Tag

Life is a collage, so when you create a celebrational tag, include a bit of everything you love.

SIZE: 2⅞" x 5"

MATERIALS:
Grafix Clear Dura-Lar .007. • Cardstock • Die cut machine and tag die • Paper flower • Large pebble brad • Rub-on doodle • Ribbons • 3 Silver faux eyelets • Silver charm• Silver square paper clip • ⅛" hole punch • Adhesive

INSTRUCTIONS:
From clear Dura-Lar, die cut 2 tags and ink edges. • Trim cardstock to fit between the tags and adhere to the back tag. Adhere tags together. Punch a hole into the top of the tags. Tie ribbons through both tags. • Wrap ribbons all the way around the tag. Apply rub-ons, stickers, and faux eyelets. Attach flower with a brad. Attach charm with a paper clip.

Congrats Tag

Looking for a gift that keeps on giving? This gift tag becomes a great bookmark after the celebration - a cheery reminder of a happy day.

SIZE: 2½" x 5½"

MATERIALS:
Grafix Clear Dura-Lar .007 • Decorative papers • Die cut machine and tag die • Rub-ons • Velvet lettering • Ribbons • Rickrack • Punches (Corner rounder, Circle) • *Tsukineko* Black StazOn ink

INSTRUCTIONS:
From clear Dura-Lar die cut 2 tags and ink the edges. • Trim papers to fit between the tags and adhere to the back tag. Adhere tags together. Punch a hole into the top of the tags. Tie ribbons through both tags. • Wrap ribbon all the way around the tag. Apply rub-ons and velvet lettering.

Flower Tag

Escape the ordinary with a clear greeting tag instead of the usual card.

SIZE: 3½" x 5½"

MATERIALS:
Grafix Clear Dura-Lar .007 • Decorative papers • Cardstock • Die cut machine and tag die • Paper flowers • Large brad • Rub-on doodles • Ribbons • *Tsukineko* Black StazOn ink • ⅛" hole punch • Adhesive

INSTRUCTIONS:
From clear Dura-Lar, die cut 2 tags and ink the edges. • Trim papers to fit between the tags, ink edges and adhere to the back tag. Adhere tags together. Punch a hole into the top of the tags. Tie ribbons through both tags. • Wrap and adhere ribbon all the way around the tag. Attach flowers to the tag front with a brad. Cut a leaf from Green cardstock; apply doodles and rub-on, "Hi." Adhere leaf to tag. • Ink the edges of the entire tag.

Special Sentiments

by Janice Musante

Let It Snow Card

Capture the sparkle of a crisp winter's night on a card that glitters with the beauty of the season.

SIZE: 4½" x 5", Envelope: 6" x 6¼"

MATERIALS:

Grafix Dura-Lar, .007; Rub-On • Stickers • Rub-ons • *Delta* Acanthus background stamp • *Tsukineko* (VersaMagic Sea Breeze; StazOn White Cotton Opaque) • *Grafix* Printable Rub-Onz • Computer

INSTRUCTIONS:

Card: Cut Dura-Lar, fold to form card and ink edges. • Stamp design on card front. Adhere jeweled snowflakes over the cover and inside the card. Computer print 3 "Let it Snow" sentiments on Rub-Onz and adhere inside card.

Love One Another Card

Gorgeous turquoise stones mix with delicate swirls on a card that is fabulous for an engagement or wedding.

SIZE: 5" x 5", Envelope: 6" x 6¼"

MATERIALS:

Grafix (Clear Dura-Lar .007, Double Tac) • Beads • Paper flowers • Ribbon • Acrylic sentiment • Rub-ons • Brads • *Delta* Acanthus background stamp • *Tsukineko* StazOn White Cotton Opaque ink • *Martha Stewart Crafts* Aqua ink • ⅛" hole punch • Double-sided tape

INSTRUCTIONS:

Card: Cut Dura-Lar, fold to form card and ink edges. • Stamp design on card front. Apply tape to left side of card, sprinkle beads and press to secure. • Attach flowers to center of card with a brad. Tape beads to flower center. Adhere ribbon under flower. Apply rub-on sentiment. Adhere sticker to inside of card.

Envelope: Ink edges of envelope. Adhere ribbon and apply rub-on words. Attach the ribbon and two paper flowers to the envelope with a large, flat head, aqua brad. Tape beads over brad.

BBQ Invitation

You're Invited to a Bar-B-Q! Bring your appetite and join us for some old-fashioned summer fun.

SIZE: 5½" x 5½", Envelope: 6" x 6¼"

MATERIALS:
Grafix Dura-Lar .007 • Decorative papers • Cardstock • Ribbon • Pebble brad • Die cuts • *Tsukineko* StazOn inks (Dew Drop, Mediterranean Blue) • Adhesives

INSTRUCTIONS:
Card: Cut Dura-Lar, fold to form card and ink edges. • Trim paper to fit card and adhere to the bottom front and bottom inside. • Cut out four 3" letter B's, 2 in reverse. Cut out four 1½" letter B's and 4 letter Q's, 2 of each in reverse. Ink all edges. Adhere 1 set of letters, die cut vines and flowers to front of card and 1 set to the inside, aligning the designs. Adhere the reverse cut letters to the backs of each page of the card, aligning the letters. • Attach a ribbon to the card front with a brad.
Envelope: Make an envelope using the template. Fold and adhere the sides to form the envelope. Line the envelope with the striped paper. Cut a strip of paper, ink edges and adhere to the bottom edge of the envelope. Adhere a die cut vine and flower.

Flag Card

by Kimber McGray
Create a clever card with striped ribbon.

SIZE: 4" x 5"

MATERIALS: *Grafix* Dura-Lar, .007 • Decorative papers • *Tsukineko* StazOn Black ink • *Pageframe* Clear star • *Cuttlebug* template and machine • Striped ribbon • Sewing machine • Adhesive

INSTRUCTIONS: Cut Dura-Lar, fold to form a card and ink the edges. • Trim paper to fit card and attach to inside. Cut and zig zag stitch ribbons to the front. Attach star.

TIP: Emboss a star between a Cuttlebug template. Cut out the star.

TIP: Apply StazOn ink to the surface of star. Wipe ink off embossed image.

Happy Birthday Girl

The colors are all girl, but the bold graphics are definitely grown up on this striking card.

SIZE: 5" x 5"
Envelope: 6" x 6¼"
MATERIALS:
Grafix Clear Dura-Lar .007
• Decorative papers • Die cuts
• Large pebble brad • Rub-ons
• Brads • Envelope template
• *Tsukineko* VersaMagic Persimmon ink • Adhesives
INSTRUCTIONS:
Card: Cut Dura-Lar, fold to form card and ink edges. • Cut printed paper into rectangles; ink edges. Apply rub-on lettering to the rectangles and adhere to card. Adhere die cuts.
Envelope: Make an envelope using the template. Cut a paper liner and adhere inside envelope. Attach paper rectangle to corner with brads. Apply sticker.

Party Time

by Janice Musante

Get Up and Party!

The confetti is already falling on this delightful invitation brimming with the promise of an energetic and lively time to be shared.

SIZE: 5½" x 5½"
Envelope: 6" x 6¼"
MATERIALS:
Grafix Dura-Lar, .007 • Decorative papers • Stickers • Vellum envelope
• *Tsukineko* VersaMagic Peach ink
• Large brads • Computer • Printer
• Adhesives
INSTRUCTIONS:
Card: Cut Dura-Lar, fold to form card and ink edges. • Trim paper to fit card and attach to the inside with brads. Apply rub-on "Smile" sentiment. Computer print "Get up and Party" and adhere inside card.
• Adhere stickers randomly over the outside of the card.
Envelope: Cut a strip of paper and adhere to the bottom edge of the envelope. Apply stickers.

A Special Wedding
by Janice Musante

Bridal Shower Invitation

Simple, classy, elegant - create an invitation as special as the event you are celebrating.

SIZE: 5" x 5½", Envelope: 6" x 6¼"

MATERIALS:

Grafix Clear Dura-Lar .005 • Cardstock • Vellum • Adhesive vellum • Ribbons • Stickers • Rub-on Doodles • *ColorBox* Black ink

INSTRUCTIONS:

Card: Cut Dura-Lar, fold to form card and ink edges. • Computer print invitation on vellum and cut out. Mat on cardstock and adhere inside card. Add rub-ons. Adhere folded ribbon and flower sticker to front of card. Adhere ribbons to the bottom edge on the back of the card front and inside.

Envelope: Make envelope using the template. Fold and tape envelope edges. Add ribbon on each side. Adhere a folded ribbon and daisy sticker.

Daisy Napkin Ring

Whether you are celebrating a wedding or just having friends over for luncheon, pretty table decorations add something special that your guests will appreciate.

SIZE: 1⅝" x 6⅛"

MATERIALS:

Grafix Clear Dura-Lar, size .005 • Sticker • Ribbons • Rub-on Doodles • Clear double-sided tape

INSTRUCTIONS:

Cut a 1⅝" x 6½" strip of Dura-Lar. Adhere ribbon to long edges. Randomly rub on doodles. Roll to form a napkin ring and secure with tape. Adhere folded ribbon and flower sticker.

Daisy Place Card

Make everyone feel welcome and guide your guests to their seats with beautifully handcrafted place cards.

SIZE: 2" x 3¾"

MATERIALS:

Grafix Clear Dura-Lar .005 • Daisy dimensional stickers • Black glitter lettering • Rub-on Doodles • Ribbons • Adhesive

INSTRUCTIONS:

Cut a 3¾" x 3¾" square of Dura-Lar. Adhere ribbon all around the edge. Fold the place card in half. Apply rub-ons and name letters. Adhere folded ribbon and flower sticker.

Handmade Envelopes

Make unique and beautiful envelopes to send with your fabulous clear cards.

SIZE: 6" x 6¼" (for 5" x 5½" cards)

MATERIALS:

Grafix Clear Dura-Lar .005 (7½" x 13½") • Adhesive

INSTRUCTIONS:

Trace the pattern onto clear film with a ballpoint pen or a grease pencil (the grease will rub off later). Cut out the shape. Score and fold the clear film with a bone folder. Crease the folds with the bone folder. Glue flaps with Diamond Glaze or Glossy Accents.

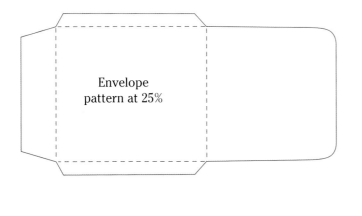

Envelope
pattern at 25%

Love Card

Tempus fugit - time flies. This old Latin saying reminds us to take advantage of the moment. In this case, make the card and send it out now. It only takes a moment to make someone smile all day.

SIZE: 4¼" x 5½", Envelope: 6" x 6¼"

MATERIALS:
Grafix Dura-Lar.005 or .007 • Photo • Decorative papers • Cardstock • Paper Flower with large pebble brad • Rub-ons • Ribbons • Epoxy sentiment • Brad • Die cut

INSTRUCTIONS:
Cut Dura-Lar, fold to form card and ink edges. • Mat a photo and adhere inside the card. Attach flower and folded ribbons inside card with a brad. Apply rub-ons and stickers.

Hall Pass

A fabulous embellishment, this Hall Pass makes a great bookmark.

SIZE: 3½" x 7"

MATERIALS:
Grafix Clear Dura-Lar .005 • Decorative papers • Die cut machine and tag die • Ribbon • Rub-ons • Paper flower • Pebble brad • *Tsukineko* Black StazOn ink • Black pen • Sharpie Permanent Black marker • Hole punch

INSTRUCTIONS:
From clear Dura-Lar, die cut 2 tags and ink edges. • Attach flower to tag front with brad. Trace the bottom portion of the tag on paper and cut two; adhere back to back. Ink edges and adhere to the back of the tag, covering the brad posts. Adhere tags together, sandwiching the paper. • Adhere ribbons around tag. Apply rub-ons. • Punch a hole in the top and thread ribbons. Knot. • Using a permanent Black marker or rub-on lettering, write out "Pass".

School Days Photo Card

Grandparents and friends always look forward to receiving the latest school photo. Share yours with this fun card.

SIZE: 5" x 5½", Envelope: 6" x 6¼"

MATERIALS:
Grafix Clear Dura-Lar .007 • Decorative papers • School photograph • Rub-ons • Large pebble brad • School stickers • Ribbons • *Tsukineko* Black StazOn ink

INSTRUCTIONS:
Card: Cut Dura-Lar and fold to make a card. Ink the edges. • Cut paper to fit inside of the card and ink edges. Mat a photo and adhere to paper. Adhere inside card. Apply rub-ons and stickers. Attach folded ribbons with a brad. Adhere ribbons and rub-ons to the card front.
Envelope: Make an envelope using a template; fold and tape edges. • Adhere ribbon along edges.

School Days

by Janice Musante

Pencil Box

Come to class prepared with this cool pencil box.

SIZE: 2½" x 8½"

MATERIALS:
Purchased clear pencil box • Ribbons • Rub-ons • Double-sided tape

INSTRUCTIONS:
Adhere ribbons around the top and bottom of the box. Apply rub-on for name. Thread ribbons through the hole in the top and knot.

Teacher Name Plate

Begin the school year with a proper introduction that helps everyone remember the teacher's name.

SIZE: 2" x 8½"

MATERIALS:
Grafix Clear Dura-Lar .007 • Decorative papers • *Ellison Press* and Apple Name Plate die • Sticker • Rub-ons • *Tsukineko* StazOn Black ink • *DecoArt* acrylic paint (Red, Brown, Green) • Sponge • Adhesive

INSTRUCTIONS:
Die cut one apple name plate from clear Dura-Lar; fold and ink edges.
• Sponge paint the apple. Let dry. • Apply rub-ons and sticker border to the bottom edge of the name plate front. • Trim paper to fit and adhere inside.

Thanks Teacher Tag

Teachers make an important difference in our lives. Take a moment to acknowledge their hard work and dedication with a great gift for Teacher Appreciation Day or any day.

SIZE: 3½" x 5½"

MATERIALS:
Grafix Clear Dura-Lar .005 • Decorative papers • Die cut machine and tag die • Stickers • Ribbon • Rub-ons • Paper flower with large pebble brad • Sharpie Permanent Black marker • *Tsukineko* Black ink • Hole punch

INSTRUCTIONS:
From clear Dura-Lar die cut 2 tags and ink edges.
• Attach flower to tag front with brad. Trace the bottom portion of the tag on paper and cut two; adhere back to back. Ink edges and adhere to the back of the tag, covering the brad posts. Adhere tags together, sandwiching the paper. • Adhere ribbons around tag. Apply rub-ons and stickers. • Punch a hole in the top and thread ribbons. Knot. • Using a permanent Black marker, handwrite "Thanks Teacher" on one side and "Teacher" on the back.

Happy Holidays

by Janice Musante

Noel Card

Send your Greetings in a card that is simply lovely.

SIZE: 4" x 5", Envelope: 6" x 6¼"

MATERIALS:
Grafix Clear Dura-Lar .007 and .005 • Ribbon • Rub-on • Envelope template • Christmas stamps (*Inkadinkado; PaperArtsy*) • *Tsukineko* ink (StazOn Black, Brilliance Gold) • *Ranger* Adirondack alcohol inks (Currant, Meadow) • ⅛" hole punch • Transparent double-sided tape

INSTRUCTIONS:
Card: Cut Dura-Lar and fold to make a card. Ink the edges. • Stamp design on the card front, let dry. • On the inside of the card, randomly drop alcohol inks. Let dry. • Apply rub-ons over the alcohol ink design. • Punch 2 holes on the card cover along the left edge and thread ribbon. Knot.
Envelope: Make an envelope using a template; fold and tape edges. • Adhere ribbon along the edges and flap. Apply rub-on snowflake.

Stained Glass Card

Stained glass is always in style for a friendly greeting.

SIZE: 4" x 5"

MATERIALS:
Grafix Clear Dura-Lar .007 • Black glitter letters • *Craft House Corp.* (Translucent gel stains: Green, Pink, Purple, White, Yellow; Squeezers) • *All Night Media* Spiral Frame stamp • *Tsukineko* StazOn Black ink • *DecoArt* Green Translucent Peel and Stick-on paint • Acrylic blank • Paintbrush

INSTRUCTIONS:
Card: Cut Dura-Lar and fold to make a card. Stamp spiral frame onto the front of the card. Ink the edges. • Paint the design using translucent gel stains. Let dry.
Inside: Adhere "hi" stickers. Drop Green paint onto acrylic blank to form dots and let dry. Peel dots and apply to the inside center of the card around the sentiment.

Snowmen Card

Send snowy greetings with a snowman card that celebrates the wonder of the season.

SIZE: 5" x 7", Envelope: 6" x 6¼"

MATERIALS:
Grafix Clear Dura-Lar .007 • White envelope • Aluminum foil • Ribbon • 3 Red poinsettias • Brads • Rubber stamps (*Stamps Happen* Festive Snowmen, *Stampendous!* Sentiment) • *Tsukineko* StazOn ink (Jet Black, Rocket Red Brilliance) • *Kelly's Crafts* Translucent gel stains (Green, Red, Opaque White, Yellow) • ⅛" hole punch • Double-sided tape

INSTRUCTIONS:
Card: Cut Dura-Lar and fold to make a card. Ink the edges. Set aside. • Stamp Festive Snowmen on a piece of Dura-Lar; paint with translucent gel stains and Opaque White paint. Let dry and cut out design. • Cut a 3" x 7" piece of foil; crunch and unfold. Trim the foil to fit beneath the stamped snowmen. Lay the painted snowmen design over the aluminum foil and adhere to card front with brads. • Attach flowers and folded ribbons with brads. • Apply rub-on sentiment inside card.
Envelope: Tape ribbons along the bottom edge of the envelope. Adhere flower and leaf with a brad.

Poinsettia Card

Wishing you Noel, Love, Joy and Peace this holiday season.

SIZE: 5" x 7", Envelope: 6" x 6¼"

MATERIALS:
Grafix Clear Dura-Lar .007 • Decorative papers • White envelope • Rub-ons • Ribbon • Brads • *Tsukineko* Brilliance Rocket Red ink • ⅛" hole punch • Adhesive

INSTRUCTIONS:
Card: Cut Dura-Lar and fold to make a card. Ink the edges. • Rub-on poinsettias strip along the lower edge of the card front. Adhere a Green paper strip along the bottom edge inside the card. Add ribbons and brads. Rub-on Gold snowflakes randomly across the Green paper. Rub-on the Gold, NOEL LOVE JOY PEACE across the top of the card. Rub-on glitter holly.
Envelope: Adhere a strip of paper, ribbon, and rub-ons along the lower front edge of the envelope. Use the envelope as a template to cut out a liner from the printed paper. Ink the edges and adhere to the inside of the envelope.

Santa Card

Send a classic greeting with this traditional Santa image on a clearly wonderful card.

SIZE: 4" x 5", Envelope: 6" x 6¼"

MATERIALS:
Grafix Dura-Lar .007 • Poinsettias w/ Leaves and Brads • Stick on letters • Snowflake sticker • *Inkadinkado* Christmas stamp • *Tsukineko* inks (Black StazOn, Brilliance Rocket Red) • *Kelly's Crafts* Green Glass Stain • Ribbon • Clear double-sided tape

INSTRUCTIONS:
Card: Cut Dura-Lar and fold to form a card. Ink edges with Red. • Stamp design on front of card in Black ink. • On the backside of the cover, pour Green ink stain over the design. Let dry. • Cut ribbons, fold in half and adhere to card with a brad in the center of a poinsettia. • Adhere "JOY" sticker letters inside card.
Envelope: Cut envelope from clear Dura-Lar using a template. Fold and adhere edges using double-sided tape. Adhere snowflake sticker and rhinestone to envelope.

Winter's Night Card

How do you have a wonderful winter? Just add snow! Capture the luster of the moon on the breast of the new fallen snow with this glittering card.

SIZE: 5" x 7", Envelope: 5¼" x 7¼"

MATERIALS:
Grafix Clear Dura-Lar .007 • White envelope

• Ribbons • Rub-ons • Stickers • Sentiment on vellum • *Tsukineko* Brilliance Galaxy Gold ink

INSTRUCTIONS:
Card: Cut Dura-Lar and fold to make a card. Ink the edges. • Apply rub-ons to card front. • Punch 2 holes, each 1" from the side of the card front and 2" from the top edge. Thread ribbon through the holes, tie and trim edges. • Apply rub-ons inside card. Rub-on one glitter snowperson along the bottom edge of the snow scene.
Envelope: Cut the vellum sentiment, "just add snow" to fit the left side of the envelope and adhere. Adhere ribbon and trim edges. Rub-on a glitter snowperson and apply snowflake stickers.

Adhesives ... How to Use Them

Diamond Glaze
Very clear and makes a fine thin line of glue. It works best with flat and paper accents.

Glossy Accents
Makes a clear line with a bit of bulk. Works best with flat paper accents and ribbon.

Fusion - Adhesive
squeezes out in a nice line with a bit of bulk. It works well with paper and silk flowers.

E6000 & Goop
Tube glues squeeze out in small pads of glue that work with dimensional accents.

Zots - Handy pads of
glue are available on a strip of tape. Position them, then adhere almost anything.

Double-sided Tape
Easy to use when it is in a tape dispenser, has great adhesion, especially for paper and film.

Pink Sticky Tape
A great tape for adhering everything from paper and flowers to glitter and micro beads.

Scrapbook Tape
Scrapbook Adhesive is available in a line of clear tape. it works great with photos and paper accents.

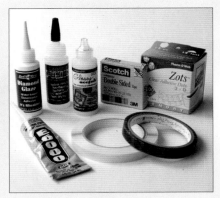

Clear Adhesives for Clear

It is important to adhere items to clear cards with special clear adhesives. We tested many glues and adhesives for adhesion and clarity. Listed below are favorites.

Diamond Glaze	*by JudiKins*
Fusion	*by Duncan*
Glossy Accents	*by Ranger*
Double-Stick Tape	*by Scotch*
Zots	*by ThermoWeb.*
E6000 or Goop	*by Eclectic*
Scrapbook Adhesive	*by 3L.*
Pink Terrific Tape	*by Provo Craft*

Colorful Cards

by Michele Charles

Happy Card

Happy Birthday! If unique is what you seek, here's a card created with no paper at all.

SIZE: 5" x 6"

MATERIALS:
Grafix Dura-Lar .007 • Brads • *Hero Arts* Stamps • *Ranger* (Glossy Accents; Adirondack Paint Dabbers: Juniper, Watermelon, Pink Sherbet) • Sharpie Hot Pink marker • *We R Memory Keepers* Crop-A-Dile

INSTRUCTIONS:
Paint back of card front. Let dry. • Stamp images with Paint Dabbers on card front. Let dry. • Punch holes in each corner. Insert brads. Cover brads and Happy words with Glossy Accents. Let dry. Paint back of card. Let dry. • Stamp 'happy' inside of card with Paint Dabbers. Let dry. Write 'Birthday' with Sharpie.

Let's Have Some Fun Card

Whether you are going out to a movie or having friends over to watch the game, this is a Fun invitation.

SIZE: 5" x 6"

MATERIALS:
Grafix Dura-Lar .007 • Cardstock (Green, White) • *Hero Arts* Stamps • *Tsukineko* StazOn inks (Black, Fuschia) • Sharpie markers • Adhesive

INSTRUCTIONS:
Stamp FUN in Fuschia ink and Butterflies in Black ink on front of card. • Color on back side of stamped images with Sharpie markers. • Tear White cardstock and adhere to back of card front. Adhere Green cardstock on inside of card. Write 'Let's Have Some' in Black Sharpie on Green cardstock.

Dream Sing Laugh Card

Words of encouragement are always welcome. Make this card for a friend or keep it for yourself.

SIZE: 5" x 6"

MATERIALS:
Grafix Dura-Lar .007 • White cardstock • Stencils • Eyelets • Rubber stamps (*Paper Bag Studios, Stampers Anonymous*) • *Tsukineko* StazOn (Teal, Blazing Red, Mustard, Black) • *Ranger* Cut n' Dry • *We R Memory Keepers* Crop-A-Dile • Adhesive

INSTRUCTIONS:
Apply Teal, Blazing Red, and Mustard inks with Cut n' Dry foam to back of card front. • Using Black ink on card front, stamp girls and wings and stencil the words. • Punch holes and attach cardstock to back of card front with eyelets. Apply inks to the back of the card as you did with the card front. Adhere cardstock to back.

1. Apply colors of StazOn inks to clear card.

2. Stamp a background image with Black StazOn ink.

3. Stamp words and images on film with Black StazOn ink.

4. Color back of image film with a White paint pen.

Mount Perfectly Clear flower stamps by *Stampendous* on an acrylic handle. Stamp flowers on cardstock and printed cardstock with Versafine Vintage Sepia ink.

Cut out the flowers. Apply a pink sticker to the center of each large cardstock flower. Apply a silver dot sticker to the center of every flower.

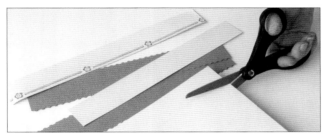

Cut strips of paper to fit around the pail and ink the edges. Wrap papers around the pail and secure the ends. Adhere photo, flowers, stickers and ribbons.

Picture Pail

by Lisa Hindsley

Store your keepsakes and memories in style with a personalized pail.

SIZE: 4½" x 5" tall

MATERIALS:
Stampendous (Tin Pail with handle; Perfectly Clear stamps: Floral Flourish, Happy Flowers; Acrylic handle for clear stamps; Class A' Peels stickers: Pink Floral Centers, Silver Dot Sparklers; Sticky Squares) • Photo • Decorative papers • Ribbons • *Provo Craft* Circles Coluzzle, Guarded Swivel Knife • *Tsukineko* Versafine Vintage Sepia Ink • Watercolors • Make-up sponge • Adhesive

INSTRUCTIONS:
Pail: Trim and mat photo. Ink the edges. • Stamp and cut out flowers. Apply stickers. Cut strips of paper to fit around the pail and ink the edges. Wrap papers around the pail and secure the ends. Adhere photo, flowers, stickers and ribbons.
Lid: Cut paper circles, ink the edges and layer on lid. Layer flowers and stickers. Adhere to lid.

Flower Tag

by Kim Moreno

Dress up a card, a gift or a scrapbook page with a unique identifying tag.

SIZE: 3" x 5"

MATERIALS:
Pageframe Designs Clear tag • Decorative paper • Flowers • Rhinestones • Ribbons • Eyelets • Slick Writer - Black • Permopaque pen - Orange • Souffle marker - Pink, Green • *We R Memory Keepers* Crop-A-Dile • Adhesive

INSTRUCTIONS:
Tie colored ribbon to the top of the tag. • Trim paper to fit and attach it with eyelets behind the tag. • Draw dots and doodles freehand with Souffle pens. Adhere flowers and rhinestones to the front of the tag.

1. Attach eyelets with the center of a Crop-a-Dile tool.

2. Draw dots and doodles with Souffle pens and a White Permopaque.

3. Adhere flowers and rhinestones. Add words with a Black Slick Writer.

Clear Ornaments
by Kim Moreno

TIP: Coat a clear item with *JudiKins* Diamond Glaze. Sprinkle glitter on surface to make it silver. Allow to dry.

TIP: Add dimensional dots to clear plastic ornaments and cards with the tip of a bottle of *Ranger* Stickles. Allow to dry.

Special Markers for Clear Cards

Use pens and markers to journal, doodle, outline, penstitch and add titles. You can also add interesting color on clear cards.

It is important to mark on clear cards with special markers. We tested many markers and pens for adhesion and opacity. Listed below are our favorites.

Slick Writers for Journaling	*by American Crafts*
Souffle Pens for Doodling	*by American Crafts*
Opaque Stix	*by Marvy-Uchida*
Permopaque Pens for Doodling	*by Sakura*
Sharpie Pens - Ultra fine point	*by Sanford*
Sharpie Pens - Fine point	*by Sanford*
Sharpie Pens - Metallics, fine tip	*by Sanford*
Sharpie Paint Pens	*by Sanford*
DecoColor - Fine tip	*by Marvy-Uchida*

Tips for Drawing and Writing with Markers

Trace Patterns - For accurate writing, tape a pattern or word under a clear card, trace right over the pattern.

Doodling - Draw freehand scrolls, lines and marks, or you can mark through plastic design templates.

Souffle Pens - At first you won't see the Souffle ink. Be patient and after a minute color will appear. It's like magic.

Slick Writers - These pens have fine tips and make wonderful marks. They are great for sentimental notes.

"Believe" Bell Ornament

by Vicki Chrisman
Ring in the holiday season with an elegant bell ornament.

SIZE: 4" x 5"

MATERIALS:
2 *Pageframe Designs* Acrylic Bell shapes • Vellum • Ribbons • Lace • Metal embellishments • Rhinestone • *Crafty Secrets* Heartwarming Vintage stamp • *Tsukineko* Black StazOn ink • *Sakura* Stardust gel pen • *Ranger* Silver foil Memory tape

INSTRUCTIONS:
Stamp images on vellum and let dry. Outline the image with a Stardust gel pen and let dry. • Lay clear bell shape over the top, centering image. Trace and cut. Sandwich the stamped vellum between 2 clear bells. Adhere with Silver Memory Tape, starting at the top of the bell so the ribbon will cover the spot where the pieces meet. Work around, smoothing with your fingers as you go. • Add ribbons, a wire swirl and rhinestone.

1. Stamp images on vellum with StazOn ink and let dry.

2. Outline the image with a Stardust gel pen and let dry.

3. Lay a clear bell shape over the top, centering the image. Cut out the shape.

4. Sandwich the stamped vellum between two clear bell shapes.

5. Adhere the bells by wrapping Silver tape around the edge.

6. Add ribbons, a wire swirl and rhinestones.

Happy Hangings

by Vicki Chrisman

Lyndsay Frame

Curled paper flowers form a shape reminiscent of a Hawaiian lei evoking a sense of endless summer.

SIZE: 6⅜" x 6½"

MATERIALS:
Pageframe Designs Clear acrylic frame 6" x 6" • Decorative papers • *AccuCut* Die cuts • Metal bookplate • Stickers • Clip • Buttons • Twill • *Karen Foster* stamps • *ColorBox* fluid ink • Pencil • *3L* Scrapbook Adhesive

INSTRUCTIONS:

Background: Layer decorative papers and photo. Slide into frame.

Frame: After inking the flower edges, curl up the petals using a pencil. Adhere initial, flowers and buttons to the frame. Add a clear epoxy embellishment over the monogram letter. Thread twill through the frame and knot to make a hanger.

Beautiful Frame

Create an interesting background and add simple embellishments for a frame that is truly Beautiful.

SIZE: 6" x 6½"

MATERIALS:
PageFrame Designs Clear acrylic frame 6" x 6" • Decorative papers • Rub-ons • Flower • Brads • Ribbon • Chipboard • Stickers • *ColorBox* fluid ink • Sewing machine • *3L* Scrapbook Adhesive

INSTRUCTIONS:

Background: Cut wavy strips of paper and weave them together before machine stitching them down. Apply rub-ons to the photo. Slide background into the frame.

Frame: Ink the chipboard corner to coordinate with your papers. Adhere flower, words and chipboard corner to the frame. Thread ribbon through the frame and tie for a hanger.

Flower and Tags Frame

Tell your story on tags attached to the hanger! What a wonderful way for your children and grandchildren to develop an understanding of who you are.

SIZE: 8" x 8½"

MATERIALS:
PageFrame Designs Clear acrylic frame 8" x 8" • Decorative papers • Chipboard letters • Lace • Buttons • Rhinestone • Ribbons • Metal rings • *Plaid* paint • *ColorBox* Black fluid ink • Black marker • Tag punch • Wax paper • Sewing machine • *JudiKins* Diamond Glaze Adhesive
**Photo by Becky Novacek

INSTRUCTIONS:
Background: Squirt some of each paint color onto wax paper. Cut out coordinating background papers and drag the edges through different colors of paint. Let dry. • Cut out and adhere flower petals, stem and leaves. Outline them with a broken line using a Black marker. • Zigzag stitch as desired. • Slide the background into the frame.
Frame: Adhere rhinestone and chipboard letters with Diamond Glaze.
Hanger: Print words for tags on paper and punch out. Paint the edges. Let dry. Ink the edges. Thread lace and ribbon through the frame and tie in a bow. Attach tags to metal rings and pin to the hanger.

TIP: Layer papers, photo and die cut. Slide the decorated page into a clear frame.

TIP: Bend a clear butterfly shape. Adhere butterfly to the front of the frame with E6000 glue.

Small Frame with Butterfly
by Kim Moreno
Rhinestones and glitter on a frame that sparkles.

SIZE: 6" x 6¼"

MATERIALS:
Pageframe Designs (6" x 6" frame, Clear butterfly shape) • Decorative papers • Cardstock • Die cut • Adhesive rhinestones • Letter stickers • *Autumn Leaves* stamps (Flourish, Love) • *Tsukineko* StazOn White ink • Glitter glue

INSTRUCTIONS:
Layer papers, photo, and die cut. Add butterfly jewel. Slide page into the frame. • Bend butterfly shape. Apply glitter glue to edge of butterfly. Add a small strip of adhesive rhinestones along the butterfly center and adhere to the front of the frame. • Stamp the word "love" above the butterfly leaving room for the letter stickers. Stamp a flourish to the left of the butterfly along the bottom of the frame. Adhere rhinestones and letter stickers.

Happy Hangings

"I Love You Mia"

by Michelle Van Etten
It's not the usual square frame! Adhering papers to the outside of the frame changes its shape for a fabulous designer look.

SIZE: 12" x 12"

MATERIALS:

Pageframe Designs 12" x 12" frame
• 11½"diameter chipboard flower
• Decorative papers • Lace • Stickers
• Transparency • Rub-ons • Chipboard letters • *ColorBox* Dark Brown fluid ink
• Crystal glitter glue • Adhesive

INSTRUCTIONS:

Outside Frame: Trace the chipboard flower on a 12" x 12" sheet of Dark Brown paper. Cut the scallop from the center, saving the outside edges for the frame. Using a 12" x 12" sheet of Pink paper, cut out a 9½" circle from the center and adhere to the frame. Adhere the Brown cutout edges, creating a scallop edged circle. Adhere rhinestones around the center. Add small photos, paper flowers, rhinestones, and chipboard letters. Decorate letters with glitter glue.
Background: Adhere papers to the chipboard flower in a patchwork design. Adhere photo and place behind the open circle of the frame. Secure to back of frame with tape.

Best Friends

by Vicki Chrisman
"Tilly & The Wall" - Derek Presnall, Jamie Presnall, Kiana Alarid, Neely Jenkins, and Nick White of Omaha, Nebraska sing tales of dreams followed, mistakes made, and hearts broken. Whether you know the band or are just a fan, create a frame that celebrates your love of music.

**Photo of the band by Keith Jenkins

SIZE: 6⅜" x 6¾"
MATERIALS:
PageFrame Designs acrylic frame 6" x 6" • Decorative papers • Lace • Clothespins
• Chain for hanging • Metal embellishments • Tiles • Sticker letters • Buttons
• *ColorBox* fluid inks (Chestnut Roan, Charcoal Black) • Double-sided tape
INSTRUCTIONS:
Mount photo and slide into the frame. • To make the dimensional flower, cut two whimsical flowers, one from paper and one from sheet music. Ink edges of both slightly. Using a pencil, curl up edges of each petal. Add button for center.
• Adhere paper strips to clothespins and adhere to the top of the frame. Add letters to scrabble tiles and adhere tiles to tops of clothespins. • Attach lace to backside of frame, allowing to hang below frame. • Tie chain in a knot, with metal washer at the top.

Original Ornaments

Holiday Ornaments
by Michelle Van Etten
Create personalized ornaments
with photos of the family to share.

SIZE: 3⅜" x 5"

MATERIALS:
PageFrame Designs Clear acrylic ornaments
• Decorative papers • Rub-ons • Ribbon
• Flowers • Eyelets • *Ranger* Crystal Stickles
• *ColorBox* Dark Brown chalk ink • Silver leafing pen • Eyelet tools • *We R Memory Keepers*
Crop-A-Dile • Adhesive

INSTRUCTIONS:
Trace the ornament on the back of a decorative paper and cut out. • Cut out the center for photo and adhere photo to the back of the ornament. Adhere paper to the back of the ornament. • Outline ornament edges with a Silver pen. Apply rub-ons, ribbon, and attach felt flowers with an eyelet.

Cutie Pie
by Kim Moreno
Simply sweet, this is my "Cutie Pie".

SIZE: 8" x 8"

MATERIALS:
Pageframe Designs Clear Flower shape
• Decorative papers • Small flowers • Rub-ons
• Adhesive rhinestones • Eyelets • Ribbons
• Eyelet tools • Crop-A-Dile tool • Adhesive

INSTRUCTIONS:
Cut a photo mat and adhere to the back of the frame. Adhere photo to the front of the frame.
• Apply rub-ons and rhinestones to the front of the frame. • Punch 2 holes in each of the flower petals and set eyelets. Tie ribbon through each set of eyelets.

1. Cut a photo mat and adhere to the back of the frame.

2. Adhere photo to the front. Apply rub-ons and rhinestones.

3. Punch holes and tie ribbon through the holes.

Wedding Memories Frame
by Michelle Van Etten

Twinkling H2Os add sparkle to your decorative papers, and a personal touch to the project.

SIZE: 11½" x 11½"

MATERIALS:
Pageframe Designs large scallop frame • Decorative papers
• Butterfly rubber stamp • Chipboard letters • Crystal rhinestones
• Journaling cards • Stickers • Ribbon • *ColorBox* Dark Brown fluid
chalk • *LuminArte* Twinkling H2Os • Glitter glue • Water brush
• Label maker • Adhesive

INSTRUCTIONS:
Use Twinkling H2Os to paint the design on the decorative paper.
Trace the scallop of the frame and cut the paper to fit. Adhere paper
to the back of the frame with FabriTac. • Cut out a stamped butterfly
image, paint and add glitter. • Adhere elements to the frame.

TIP: Decorate clear film
with a rubber stamp. Cut
it out to make a unique
dimensional butterfly.

TIP: Glittery crystals and
rhinestones really look
fabulous with clear... adding
sparkle to the surface.

Glimmer - It is easy to add sparkle and a slight texture to clear cards. Spray cards with Glimmer Spray or Glitter Spray. It will look milky at first, so be sure to let it dry to clear overnight.

Boy Frame
by Vicki Chrisman

Have some fun with layered papers and create delightful effects. Though far from ordinary, this frame is simple and inexpensive to make.

SIZE: 8½" x 11"

MATERIALS:

Pageframe Designs Clear acrylic frame 8" x 11" • Decorative papers • Cardstock • Buttons • Stickers • Rickrack • Scallop die cut • Photo corner punch • *3L* Scrapbook Adhesive

INSTRUCTIONS:

Mix brightly colored papers layered with different edges, some torn, some scalloped. Add stickers and slide into frame. Adhere buttons to the outside of the frame with E6000 glue. A large photo corner acts as an arrow that directs your eye to the photo. Thread rickrack through the frame to make a hanger.

Baby Frame
by Vicki Chrisman

The photo background slides out easily, so you can update your photo for a new look.

SIZE: 8" x 8"

MATERIALS:

Pageframe Designs Clear 8" x 8" frame • Decorative papers • Cardstock • Buttons • Heart pin • Lace • Safety Pin • Chipboard letter • Scalloped die cut • *ColorBox* fluid ink • Sewing machine • *3L* Scrapbook Adhesive

INSTRUCTIONS:

Achieve a dimensional look by inking and layering papers in the background. Zigzag stitch papers as desired. Adhere buttons, lace, heart pin and chipboard letter to the outside of the frame.
• To make a decorative hanger, thread lace through the frame, tie in a bow and add a safety pin.

TIP: Drape a piece of lace blanket across the photo.

TIP: Attach buttons to the frame with E6000 adhesive.

Happy Hangings

Each Day is a Gift

by Vicki Chrisman

Each day is a gift. That's why they call it 'the present'. Create a beautiful frame to share with loved ones. Choose papers and embellishments that coordinate with your decor to make something special for your home.

**Photo by Keith Jenkins

SIZE: 8½" x 11"

MATERIALS:

Pageframe Designs Clear frame 8" x 11"
• Decorative papers
• Cardstock • Chipboard
• Rhinestones • Ribbon
• Buttons • *Karen Foster* stamps • *ColorBox* Chestnut Roan ink
• *Apple Barrel* paint
• Sewing machine
• *3L* Scrapbook Adhesive

INSTRUCTIONS:

Layer papers and Zigzag stitch as desired. Add thin chipboard embellishments and slide into the frame. Adhere thicker chipboard, buttons and rhinestones to the surface of the frame. Thread ribbons through the frame to make a hanger.

Fall leaves look fabulous in glimmery gold leaf on a clear card and envelope.

Fall Favorites

by Janice Musante

Autumn Greetings

Dripping with seasonal color, Autumn Greetings sparkles with the golden hues of harvest time.

SIZE: 5" x 6", Envelope: 5¼" x 7¼"

MATERIALS:
Grafix Dura-Lar .007 • Decorative papers • Cardstock • Gold Leaf accents • Rub-ons • Raffia • *Ranger* Adirondack alcohol inks (Caramel, Current, Meadow, Ginger, Latte) • *Tsukineko* StazOn inks (Gold, Black) • Envelope die cut • Label Maker with Black tape and Gold lettering • *Beacon* Zip Dry Paper Glue • Adhesive

INSTRUCTIONS:

Card: Fold a card from clear Dura-Lar and ink edges. • Draw a free-form swirl using Zip Dry glue on the inside of the card. Let dry. Drip alcohol inks onto the inside and front of the card. Gently smudge with a felt pad. Let dry. • Apply rub-on leaves to the card front. • Use the label maker to print "AUTUMN GREETINGS" and adhere to card. • Adhere Gold papers back to back and adhere to the back of the card. Ink all edges in Gold.

Envelope: Die cut envelope from Tan cardstock; fold and adhere edges. Cut a strip of Dura-Lar; ink edges with Black ink. Drip and smudge alcohol inks as on card. • Attach the Dura-Lar strip to the lower edge of the envelope with brads. Wrap raffia around each brad; trim. • Use the label maker to print "AUTUMN" and adhere to the Dura-Lar strip.

Kimberly Moreno

Kim has been scrapbooking for over 7 years, with features in many publications including Memory Makers, Creating Keepsakes, Scrapbook Trends, Paper Crafts and more. She is co-owner and design team coordinator for Pageframe Designs. You can see her work at www.scrapbookresumes.com/Kim Moreno/

Lisa Hindsley

As Art Director for Stampendous, Lisa is a busy designer. With an Art Education degree from Ball State University, she's taught Art in elementary through high school. Lisa writes poetry, designs greeting cards and rubber stamps, and has designed logos for a number of artists. You can see her work at www.stampendous.com.

Vicki Chrisman

Paper Crafting is Vicki's passion. Her work has been featured on covers of Altered Art and Paper Art magazines. She was Creating Keepsakes, May 2007 "Fresh Face" and designs for Scrapbook Answers magazine, Crafty Secrets Heartwarming Vintage, Fancy Pants , AccuCut, and PageFrame Designs.